Never Alone

Copyright Text @ 2015 By Mildred L. Buchanan
Copyright Cover Design @ 2015 Darian D. Day

Published in the United States by Soul Flow Publications, a division of The TMW Group Enterprises, LLC. Saint Louis, Missouri.

For more information please visit us at
www.soulflowpublications.com

Library of Congress Cataloging-in-Publication-Data
Buchanan, Mildred L
        Never Alone
Buchanan, Mildred L; Cover Design by Darian D. Day 1st Edition
        ISBN-13: 978-0-9838828-4-8 (paperback)
        LCCN: 2015953624

1st Edit: LaTonia D. Pearson
Final Edit: Mildred L. Buchanan
Cover Design: Darian D. Day

Distributed by Soul Flow Distribution, a division of The TMW Group Enterprises, LLC. Saint Louis, Missouri.

Printed in the United States via CreateSpace.

NEVER ALONE

Written

Under the unction of the Holy Ghost

By

Evangelist Mildred L. Buchanan

Then shall the dust return to the earth as it was: and the spirit unto God who gave it. Ecclesiastes 12:7 All Scriptures KJV

Dedication

To all my loved ones who have made the transition from mortal to immortal. To my loving father and mother Elmo James and Allie Mae Childs, my brothers Joe Louis and James Henry, and sister Carrie Lee Williams, I am so glad that God placed you all in my life. We have shared many experiences that make me the person I am today. I know that we only pass this way once, so I thank God for the impact not only made on me by being a part of the Childs Family, but also the others we have touched, and the lessons we learned at home on "doing unto others as we would have them do unto us." **Comfort ye, comfort ye my people, said your God. (Isaiah 40:1)**

I also thank my pastor Bishop Ronnie and his wife Evangelist Winnetta Whittier, for fostering such an encouraging and nurturing environment, in which one can grow, express themselves freely, and utilize our God-given gifts in a Christian venue.

CONTENT

WE CRY ABBA FATHER

Psalm 27:7 Hear, O Lord, when I cry with my voice: have mercy also upon me, and answer me.

When sorrow at the loss of a loved one to us comes, and the burden is too hard for us alone to bear, it is such a blessing to have others you can depend on, to this burden share. Dear family, your friends come to hold you up in prayer, as we offer you our deepest heartfelt sympathy in the loss of your loved one. We stand by your side as we beseech almighty God on your behalf. Remember, weeping may endure for a night, but joy cometh in the morning; **Psalm. 30:5b**

God never makes any mistakes and He will not leave us comfortless. He is our present help in time of need. So I adjure you to just lay your head on His shoulder and cry "Abba Father, I need You", and He promised to carry this burden for you. He admonished us in **I Peter 5:7** to cast all our care upon Him for He careth for us.

It is our prayer that God comforts and Keeps you. Remember, we are only a voice away and will respond to your call be it day or night.

WHEN WE JUST DON'T UNDERSTAND

II Timothy. 4:7 I have fought a good fight, I have finished my
course, I have kept the faith

Some times in the trials of life when
we just don't understand
This is the time we must lean on God
and allow him to take our hand
For only God in His wisdom
knows the complete plan
So He sent the Holy Ghost
to guide you and me
Thank God that when we finish
our course we too can be free

For long ago your loved one put
their hand on the gospel plow
And accepted Jesus as His Lord and
Saviour and to Him only bow
He made the decision to keep his eyes on
the prize of the high calling a long time ago
When he decided that following Jesus
was the only way he wanted to go

So after that he has climbed the
highest mountain feeling so strong
And with voice lifted up for Jesus
sang his last glorious song
He truly witnessed for the Master
all his sanctified life long
And now he has taken off this
old flesh and gone on home
Ran a good race and now his
course was finally won
So even in our sorrow we pray
God's will be done

You know he loved you and he
really didn't want to leave
But the Master was calling and
Him he always strived to please
He decided just the other day to
go on and accept his pay
He had committed his all and
allowed the Lord to have His way

Remember he hung around a
long time so we could see
And by his witness of faith in God
help strengthened you and me
Although the treasure stored in this
earthly tabernacle is no more
You have the blessed assurance you
will meet him on the distant shore

So dry your tears because he
was ready to go home
Just remember this parting
will not be very long
He had to put off mortality for
immortality and did it with a smile
And if you who will follow Jesus then
this separation will only be for a little while

HEARD A HIGHER CALL

Isaiah. 43:1 But now thus saith the Lord that created thee, O Jacob, and he that formed thee, O Israel, Fear not: for I have redeemed thee, I have called thee by thy name; thou art mine.

Comfort ye, Comfort ye my people, speak comfortingly with these words; we do not sorrow as those that have no hope. As Jesus came the first time, so will He come again. ---and the dead in Christ shall rise first: Then we which are alive and remain shall be caught up together with them in the clouds, to meet the Lord in the air: and so shall we ever be with the Lord
(I Thessalonians 4:16b, 17)

Dearly beloved sister, devoted friend, child of the Most High God, begs your indulgence for her early departure, but she had a higher call that needed her immediate attention. She heard her Master's voice and decided just the other day to go on and accept her reward. She knew that for her to live was Christ and to die gain; so sorry my leaving has caused you so much pain. She had before witnessed just a shadow of God's glory, and now she has the privilege of being summoned into His very presence.

I am sorry for you dear family, but as you surely know, death is the way all flesh must go. Weeping is O.K you see for I know you are only crying because I have stepped into eternity. Fear not for me, for with the Holy Ghost as my guide I am now kneeling by God's side (II Corinthians 5:8 ...absent from the body, and to be present with the Lord.)

11

So dear loved ones, as you must also run this holy race, then you will by faith know we will be together again when you too will see God face to face. Shed a few tears if you must, then commit yourselves to His trust. And as you also in His Word abide, remember His promise that we shall be together again on the other side if you accept Jesus as your Lord and Saviour.

The Lord inspired men to write for all to see that by the scriptures we will be set free. God revealed a long time ago, Then shall the dust return to the earth as it was: and the spirit shall return unto God who gave it. (Ecclesiastes 12:7)

So shed a few tears if you will and then keep me alive in your memories for all the good times, the sad times, for all the joy, all the happiness, and all the pains we shared, but then you must move on with your lives and serve the Lord with gladness. Remember this scripture; Blessed be God, even the Father of our Lord Jesus Christ, the Father of mercies, and the God of all comfort; Who comforteth us in all our tribulation, that we may be able to comfort them which are in any trouble, by the comfort wherewith we ourselves are comforted of God. (II Corinthians 1:3-4)

May the God of all glory, comfort and strengthen you in this your hour of sorrow.

WHAT'S BETWEEN THE DASH

Ecclesiastes. 3:1-2 To everything there is a season, and a time to
every purpose under the heaven: A time to be born, and a time to
die; a time to plant, and a time to pluck up that which is planted;

Saints had no choice of when they would be born
nothing to say about their birth even if they tried
Neither had they a choice of who their parents
would be nor a choice on when they would die
Even though those choices were made by others
and were never given to them you see
They did have a choice on what went on between
their dashes and how it affected you and me

Our lives are but a vapor lent by God that
stays around only for a short while
So what we do between our dashes can
leave good memories of a kind and gentle smile
Death is an intricate part of life and this never
changing fact is so real
No matter whom death calls be it sister
father brother or mother there is no appeal

So I will testify that life is only the beginning
of our journey to death and that's the real deal
When a man is born, he is granted only a few
years to live on this old sinful earth wherein he plods
But he is given the heart and free-will to accept the
gift of atonement that comes only from God
Really what's between the dashes of our lives is very
short and seems to pass and be over with a nod

Only God knows what the future has in
store for each and every woman or man
And He admonished us to lay up our
treasures in heaven for this is His plan
For as surely as a man is born he must
also die and will one day be raised and live again
And no one knows when death will come
but we can have the victory over death and win

If you like this saint while the breath of
Life is in your body made the right choice
Because like him you will have to choose in
life for pass the grave you will have no voice
So when death steals a loved one even though
we no doubt feel the pain of this loss have no doubt
But what we do between our dashes will leave
memories of what our life was all about

Yes death is an interwoven part of all our lives
yet it causes us such sorrow and pain
But it is God's plan for there is no other
way for us to heaven gain
So all the ones who must carry the burden
of the loss of their loved one on this day
Remember if you chose Jesus in your
dash then death is only a journey through
the grave to Heaven's Pathway

TREASURE BEYOND MEASURE
Isaiah 61:3 to give unto them beauty for ashes, the oil of joy for
mourning, the garment of praise for the spirit of heaviness;

When sorry at the loss of a loved one to us come and
we are bowed down with sorrow and the burden is too
hard for us alone to bear, it is such a blessing to know
that others are praying for you as they try to of this
burden share.

Dear Family, we come to hold you up in prayer as we
offer you our deepest heartfelt sympathy in the loss of
your loved one. We stand by your side as we beseech
almighty God on your behalf. Remember that these
light afflictions are but for a moment and this acute
pain too shall pass; **II Corinthians 4:17**.

God never makes any mistakes and He will not leave
us comfortless. He is our present help in time of need.
So I adjure you to just lay your head on His shoulder
and He will comfort you and embrace you in His
loving arms throughout this storm of grief you are
going through. He promised to carry this burden for
you and take you through to a brighter tomorrow.
He admonished us to call on Him in our time of need
and He will answer and comfort you as only He can.

When you remember all those times with your loved
one, the wonderful and even the sad, these are
treasures that will forever be in the deepest recess of
your heart. You alone can pull them out and enjoy the
memories of the one who made such an impact not
only on your life, but also on those who are here
today. Keep these treasured memories alive and allow

God to handle the rest. Pull together as a family, as you continue to share the rich treasure of your sweet memories of your loved one and be thankful to God for allowing you to share in their lives.

God comfort and Keep you is our prayer, Remember we are only a call away and we will respond to your call be it day or night.

PORTRAIT OF MY MOTHER

Proverbs 31:31 Give her of the fruit of her hands; and let
her own works praise her in the gates.

Arms and a heart that were
always opened for me so wide
Humor with a smile that could
only be measured by the mile
Hands that for me always
found something to do
Love that could be counted
on to always carry me through

Lap like no other made just
for me to rest a while
As the sun always came through
because of her radiant smile
One who shared my tears built my
hopes and was my life's guide
Just when we were growing closer
you are no longer at my side

One who's light in my memory
will never completely fade
For the very essence of you will be
with me until the grave
One closer look would tell you why
she could love me and be so wise
For you see to me, my mother was
really an angel in disguise

CHERISHING THE GIFT OF A MOTHER

Matthew 6:21For where your treasure is, there will your heart be also.

The joy of hearing your voice will
no longer be heard by me
For just the other day you went
away to a place that I cannot see
The memories of your smiling face
I keep deep within my heart
And I know that I am going to
cry many tears while we are apart

I thank God for the time He gave us
to share such a wonderful person as you
My life was made better because mother
you made a difference as you passed through
You gave me something that others forgot
to give for you gave of yourself
I remember all the times you stood
by me even when there was no one else

I know we cannot hold on to anybody
when the Spirit of God calls unto them
No matter how much we loved you Mother
the soul will always answer Him
For he has warned us that the dust
must return unto the earth again
So our bodies must return to the dust
that place where our lives first begin

I want to remember that you fought
a good fight and now your rest is at hand
For God said death is an appointment from
Him given to each and every woman and man

So today we should remember to love
each other as if it is in this life our last day
For tomorrow you cannot call back
and then to your love one say
I thank God for putting you in my life
where your memories will forever stay

For tomorrow we can never be sure
of it any of us will see
So while we have today trust
in the Lord so you too will be free
And when the thief comes which is death
he will have no hold over thee
For while in this life we put our trust
in Jesus then His promise is to you and me

That we can be safe in His loving arms as
He had plans for each of our lives
Now He desires to uphold and comfort
you as He will dry your weeping eyes
Jesus feels your hurt and He knows
what it is to have a loving mother
For God created this special being
called mother that is made like no other
So dear mother although we will miss you
and will forever feel this void in our hearts
We will always keep your memories alive
for they are our legacy from you
that will never from us depart

WEEPING IS BUT FOR MOMENT
Romans 12:15 Rejoice with them that do rejoice, and weep with
them that weep

Although we always feel the pain in loss of a
loved one, but no pain can describe to loss of a dear
grandmother. With this loss, although anticipated, is
still a burden too hard for us to bear alone. So it is
such a blessing to have others you can depend on in
this, your time of need. Death is one thing that we can
never get ready for, even though we realize it is a very
intricate part of all of our life's experiences.

Knowing that death is a very real part of living
though it causes us so much pain. It is such a blessing
that we can depend on the support of others in this
time of sorrow. So we, your church family and friends
come to hold you up in prayer, as we offer you our
deepest heartfelt sympathy in the loss of your dear
grandmother, even though this is heaven's gain. We
stand by your side as we beseech almighty God on
your behalf. Remember weeping may endure for a
night but joy cometh in the morning, Psalms 30:5b.
God never makes any mistakes and He will not leave
us comfortless. He is our present help in time of need.
He promised to carry this burden for you. He informed
us in John 14:18 that He would not leave us
comfortless. He hears your every cry and is a present
help in your time of need.

Remember we are only a call away and we will
respond to your call, as we take your burden to the
Lord in prayer.

WHEN I WEEP
John 11:35 Jesus wept.

When my heart is so heavy I have to weep
Then I just run to Jesus for my tears to keep
For He knows all and my pain He surely see
For He Himself was tested on all points just like me

So as I must say goodbye to my dear great
grandmother
I will remember you for you were to me like no other
And I want to always keep the memory of love alive
As you have taught me that in love all things survive

A cry from a 9 year old grandchild's heart

HELPING YOU TO CARRY THIS HEAVY LOAD
Galatians 6:2 Bear ye one another's burdens, and so fulill the law of
Christ.

God has admonished us in His Holy Word
that it is appointed man once to die
We want to pray with you and hold you up
to our Heavenly Father if you need to cry
Even though we know at times like these
there is really nothing we can say or do
We just want you to know that we your
Christian brothers and sisters are here for you

To hold your hand and offer you our support
and our shoulders on which you can lean
For we know you are hurting and sad because
God called your love one to come on home
We don't have the memories of the times
with your loved one that you and your family had
Neither can share your growing years with him
in your life that made you so glad

But we know that the joy and tears of your
shared love will be a comfort in your memory
We know that coping with this heartache and pain
of losing your loved one is really hard to be
The tears and sorrow you feel because your loved
one stepped into eternity and had to go away
Will turn to great joy if you only remember
that God promises us a brighter day

And if you lean on Him in this your hour of sorrow
He will strengthen and carry you through
Jesus said if you accept Him while the breath
is still in your body then death can't hurt you
Then we the redeemed can loudly say oh death
where is thy sting oh grave where is your victory
For we know that our redeemer lives and
He has paid the price so that death will have no
hold over you or me

WE HAVE THE VICTORY
I Corinthians 15:55 O death, where is thy sting? O grave, where
is thy victory?

We your friends and the entire church family come to hold
you up in prayer. We offer you our deepest heartfelt
sympathy in the loss of your dear loved one.

When we lose a loved one even though we know that God is
in complete control,there is still a void in our lives that no
other can completely fill. We each have a special place in
the lives of those we touch on our journey from the cradle to
the grave. Lives were touched by your loved one so his
journey from mortality into immortality will be felt by the
many that knew and loved him

As one who understands the lost feelings of losing a loved
one We just want to remind you that God knows and He
cares He is there for you to heal and uplift you as no other
can Remember He too felt pain when His only begotten
Son died on that old rugged cross. But Jesus conquered
death for His redeemed ones **I Thessalonians 4:13…**that
ye sorrow not, even as others which have no hope. But as
those whose trust in the Lord and hope for His glorious
appearing So we wait in great anticipation for the soon
coming Bride Groom; **Revelation 22:20**

We your church family just wants you to know that
even though the miles may separate us at this time
we are only a phone call away we are praying
for you and your entire family. As the Lord
Himself undergird you with His strength in this
your time of need

THE PATHWAY TO GLORY
I Corinthians 15:26 The last enemy that shall be destroyed
is death .

The agony that death brings to each
of us that it has touched
The pain and heartache that makes
us cry Lord this is just too much
Why oh Lord does this suffering heartache
and pain never seem to end
As just the other day death came
for my husband who was also my friend

This loss seems more than any one
person should have to bear
Lord can you not see the pains
God don't You for us care
It seems like I just turned around and
you were no longer there
I cry now so hard for him for I never
got to really say goodbye
The question that I keep asking is
Lord why did he have to die

I know that one day the pain will not be
so intense when I think of you
And then I will remember with joy and
laughter the things we use to do
Then I will be able to reflect on God's
plan for it is written in His holy book
And realize that He has never made a mistake
no matter whose loved one He took

Death is an intricate part of life
yet it causes us such sorrow and pain
But it is God's plan for there is no other
way for us to heaven gain
So all who must carry the burden
of loss of their loved one on this day
Remember that death is only a journey
through the grave to Heaven's pathway

Then when on the morrow we
wake up to God's blessed face see
Then we will all rejoice because in
His presence we will forever be
And we will be so happy as loved ones
all come together again at His throne
If we accepted Jesus while in this world
then God Himself will welcome us all home

THE COMFORT THAT COME IN OUR TIME
OF NEED II Corinthians 1:3-4 Blessed be God, even
the Father of our Lord Jesus Christ, the Father of
mercies, and the God of all comfort; Who comforteth
us in all our tribulation, that we may be able to comfort
them which are in any trouble, by the comfort
wherewith we ourselves are comforted by God.

We your friends and your entire church family stand in the
gap for you in this time of sorrow. Sometimes words just will
not comfort but prayer is a far reaching arm that touches the
very heart of God. And He will uphold you with His strength
in this your time of weakness

Although death is an intricate part of life it leaves a void
that somehow lingers well past the actual event. So we will
continue to hold you and your family up in prayer now is
the time for you to draw closer together and to celebrated
the life of your loved one. To thank God for His kindness
in allowing them to be such an intricate part of your lives

Remember that there is no test taken you but such that is
common to man. Even though others have stood in this
same place and faced that old enemy death still we
sometimes feel so all alone. But I remind you of God's great
love and provisions for you, even in this time of testing.
Remember God will not allow you to be tested above that
which ye are able and with this test He will comfort and
give you peace as He makes a way of escape for you. He will
keep His   promise to you and send the comforter to hold
you up as He dries away all your tears; **Revelation 21:4**

We stand as a hand to hold or a shoulder to cry on or just a listening ear. But most of all we stand united together in prayer for you and your family Call and we will answer, but most assuredly God will answer prayer and He will comfort you as no other can

BEAR YE ONE ANOTHERS BURDEN

Matthew 25:40 And the King shall answer and say unto them,
Verily I say unto you, Inasmuch as ye have done it unto one of
the least of these my brethren, Ye have done it unto me.

When you upheld me and stood by my side
When you held my hand and wiped
my eyes while I cried
When you came and did the things
that needed to be done
When you watched and helped
comfort my loved ones

You brought a little sunshine to their
eyes as you helped them carry on
They were so grieved because I
stepped into eternity and went on home
Even with all the help you gave there is
still only One who knows their pain
And He is standing by to give them peace
with tranquility as their gain

For we know that death is an intricate
part of life that none can escape
But in eternity there is a Saviour who has paid
for your ticket into those pearly gates
Jesus is the way the truth and the life the
only way to God is salvation through Him
He waits to lead us from the grave to our mansion
because without Him the way is too dim

SHARING THE BURDEN TOGETHER
Galatians 6:2 Bear ye one another's burdens, and so fulfill the
law of Christ.

There is a time when we must all lean on others
Sorrow feels so deep and lasting
in the loss of a dear brother
God knew this from the start
so He put your burden on others hearts
To give as if we are giving unto the Lord
is the privilege of doing our part

Though we know that you will miss your loved one so
Our help to you is available we want you to know
We lend a helping hand as through
this trial you must stand
No we really cannot of all your
hurt and pain understand
But we know He said death would visit every man

So as we know God does all things for our good
We will stand in this trial with you as we should
For we know that the privilege of serving
you in your sorrow today
Will remind you that being our brother's
keeper is the Lord's way

To mourn with those who have their
abode in the house of sorrow
But not sorrowing as those who did not
have God's promised tomorrow
We will pray and uphold you as
our faith in God is tried
Knowing that on this day His comfort
will dry your weeping eyes

So lean on us as we go to God
in your stead standing in the gap for you
Rest as we remind Him of your sorrow
now so raw and to you so new
Calling on our Saviour to hear our
prayer and carry you through
Until you can stand in the strength
He will provide to you
Because we know that on the pathway
to glory the grave we must pass through

So lift up your head as on the wings of prayer
He will help you in this trial to stand
Jesus said all who labor come unto Me
nd I will give you rest even in this sinful land
He stands at the right hand of the Father
interceding for you and your family in this test
For He knew that He worked all things for your
good He did for your loved one what was best

PRAYER CHANGES THINGS
Psalm86:7 In the day of my trouble I will call upon thee:
for thou wilt answer me.

We your friends along with your entire church family bring you our deep felt sorrow at the loss of your dear cherished loved one.

We understand this loss for we too have been in this place of sorrow many times and we still feel the devastating void when our loved ones step from the natural ream into the eternal. When they pass through the veil of mortality and are beyond what our natural eyes can see, there is a sense of loss and helplessness to prevent our loved one from leaving us. But we must understand that God promised us three score and ten and by reason of strength we get more, **Psalm 90:10**.

Your loved one was very blessed to see the fourscore and then some and she witnessed many of life's changes but also to witness the faithfulness of God. God makes no mistakes and He always gives us space to come unto Him no matter how long it takes.

We may not always know why all this grief and sorrow, but one day we will understand when we see our Saviour face to face as we travel on this Halleluiah Road to our Father's house. There He will wipe away all our tears then we will see the things that he has prepared for them that love Him, **Revelation 21:4**.

One day there will be no more reasons for condolences for God Himself will wipe away all tears from our eyes. He said in His word, "Comfort ye, comfort ye, my people with my Word" as we kneel in prayer for you and lift you up to almighty God who answers His children speedily in their times of sorrow.

Family there is no better time than this for us to all draw nearer to God as we draw nearer to each other. Our prayers are with you as We kneel before Almighty God on your behalf, knowing that prayer reaches the throne of God and changes things. And prayer will give you the comfort you need at this time.

HALLELUIAH I'M FREE

Revelation 14:13And I heard a voice from heaven
saying unto me, Write, Blessed are the dead which die
in the Lord from henceforth: yea saith the Spirit, that
they may rest from their labours; and their works do
follow them.

Praise the Lord Halleluiah thank God I'm finally free
No more suffering and pain in this old body for me
I fought a good fight and I finished my course for all
to see Now I can rest for the Lord has prepared
a place for me with Him in eternity

So this little frail body you now see can in no
wise hold my spirit which is soaring so free
Death is an intricate part of life because
of sin into the world it came to be
But salvation was God's plan for me and
there is no other way for us to heaven gain
So in this life I accepted Jesus as my Saviour
and now eternal life I have obtained

For I know that death for me is only a journey
through the grave to Heaven's pathway
So on this very sad day remember that each
of you will one day have to pass death's way
For God said in His word that death is an
appointment we all must keep one day
So I just want to this day admonish each of you
to hear what about it God has to say
Give Him your lives so you will live in eternity
with Him for there is really no other way

Halleluiah praise God for His manifold
blessing for I am now completely free
And I know that God's plan and His
purpose for my life was finished you see
Halleluiah praise His holy name for Jesus paid
the ransom price and conquered death for me
For I put my hands on the gospel plow and
gave Him my life while I lived in the land
So now I have His blessed assurance that death
is only sleep for this sanctified woman

THE COMFORT THAT ONLY COME
THROUGH PRAYER

Death is an entity that invades all of our lives at one time or another. Yet even though it causes such pain because of the void left to those who must endure this heartache, still it is God's plan. And death is a never changing part of life and it will come to us one and all.

Words will never really express the feelings of those who experience this loss, but we want to remind you that prayer really does change things. So we offer up to Almighty God our heartfelt prayers on your behalf knowing that we will reach heaven from our knees.

THE COMFORT THAT ONLY COME
THROUGH PRAYER

Isaiah 40:1 Comfort ye, comfort ye my people, saith your
God

I would like to hold your hand as the tears flow
I would try to comfort you in the only way I know
If I could I would take away
all your pains and heartaches
I would try to make you understand
that God doesn't make mistakes

Then I would tell you that
this sorrow too shall pass
Try to make you see that this heart
rendering pain will not last
Then when I find that no words
of comfort will really do
Then my friend I will fall on my knees
and pray for God to carry you through

For I know that He is a present
help in our times of need
He will stand beside you when
your life does to Him please
He will be your buckler and shield
to uplift and sustain you
For dear family only God can give
us comfort as no one else can do

Praying for you and your family

WE KNOW OF WHOM WE HAVE OUR HOPE

James 5:16b The effectual fervent prayer of a righteous man
availeth much.

Man was born to live for a short time
but he also was born to die
When our loved ones pass over to
the other side we often wonder why
Lord I just don't always understand
why he had to leave this land
Death stole him without giving us a chance
to say goodbye it took him out of our hand

Now the memories that we shared over
the years will have to last us a lifetime
For he took a stroll into eternity the
other day and had to leave us all behind
You see the day he was born he had
an appointment with death that he had to keep
But we will miss him so and the pain of this
lost will many a day cause us to weep

God understands your loss for remember
His Son died too on that old rugged cross
Hold fast to He who promises to one day
wipe away all your tears and pain from this loss
Look to Him who is able to comfort you
and to carry your pains and sorrows
For God would that all would be comforted
with His promises of a brighter tomorrow

So dear loved ones cry if you must
but then gently gently let me go
For Jesus gave me the assurance
of eternal life with Him and I know it's so
When by faith I submitted my all to Him
just a short time ago for all to see
Now I've heard my Master's voice calling
saying all who labor come unto Me

For now your mansion is ready
which for you I have prepared
And there is no good thing that I
will withhold and I will meet you there
So goodbye dear loved ones remember
it's only but for a little while
See you on the morrow when we
will meet again on the other side
Until then hold your head up high
for this was God's plan
For we know that death is only sleep
for this sanctified man

GATHER TOGETHER ON THE OTHER SIDE

Ecclesiastes 12:13 Let us hear the conclusion of the
commandments: for this is the whole duty of man.

Come let us gather together and lift
our voices up high and sing
For another has left this old world
and the pain and suffering that it brings
But on the morrow there can be great
joy for each and every one of us
If we accepted that precious gift of Jesus
and to God learn to trust

For this sorrow that is yours today heaven does allow
But joy cometh in the morning if to God
we decide in this world to bow
For He alone has the keys to death and hell
and He will give unto you peaceful eternal rest
If you stand for Jesus and in His righteousness
in this life then you have passed the test

For all have sinned so our righteousness
still comes so very short of His Glory
So living for Him covered by His blood is the
only way you want to end your life's story
As one day when you will surely hear the
words time for you is no more
Then if you didn't meet Him in the air you're
sure to meet Him on yonder shores

In that glorious place that
for all saints He has prepared
When He said I will return
for you either in death or in the air
So dear loved ones hear the good news
that the Lord Jesus has made for you a way
If you accept Him in this life then with God
you may in that eternal Promised Land stay

THE FLICKERING LIGHT

I Corinthians 15:51b-52aWe shall not all sleep, but we shall all
be changed, In a moment, in the twinkling of an eye, at the last
trump.

The flickering light has gone out and all can see
The pain and heartache it has
caused unto you and me
For this light of my mother's
love was one of a kind
And it had the power so strong
That none other can so bind
Like the love that comes only through
loving a mother like mine

So you see I know that God has just
taken her as a flickering light
To place on the other side of glory
so she can there shine so bright
But to us she gave a legacy of
love that we hold so dear
To build us up in love for each other
as we feel her presence always near

When we pull together as the loving
team she meant us to be
And each of us serves the Master
so one day we too can be free
To soar in His divine presence and hear Him proclaim
That we may enter into His rest because
we trusted in Jesus' name

So to all my family this is to you my final decree
That you live a life that honors Christ for all to see
Then when you stand before that great white throne
Jesus the righteous will be your advocate to lead you
safely home

WHEN MY HEART IS OVERWHELMED

Psalm 18:6 In my distress I called upon the Lord, and cried unto
my God: he heard my voice out of his temple, and my cry came
before him, even into his ears.

How would I Oh Lord this heartache
and pain continue to bear
If I did not know that You
promised me to always be there
Some pains Oh Lord I feel
are just too much for a mother
For You know that the loss
of a child is a pain like no other

How can I who have no strength
Left in this body so weak go on
Stand up to this trial of such pain and
devastating loss on my own
All life is in Your hands and I know
that death is Your command
That it's an appointment given to all
mankind living in this land

What Oh Lord is a mother to do
when she can't stay death's hand
How can she try to lift up others so that
they may continue to stand
And see that all power is in the Master's hand
and that for you He does good
Even when we cannot see the whole plan and
at this time it's not by us understood

But the Creator God said I will one
day wipe all your tears away
For I know your pain for I too was
tested like you on that awesome day
So each tear that you shed is
precious in the Lord's sight
But He promised that He will hold
you up through this dark dreary night

And on the morrow He will make everything right
As a mother He has given you a special love so bright
That even in trials you are blessed that your light so shines
To show His love that through you
will this family together bind

Until you meet your loved one again when
that fearsome day comes around
When Jesus will the clouds part and
the angels with the trumpets sound
For all to hear and I hope that each of you
will with your mother see
God's smiling face as He said all
who accepted My Son come unto me

Remember death is only the doorway
that we must all pass through
It is the way that God designed things
for each and every one of you
But believe me this is not by
any means the end of anything
For it's really just the beginning
of our new life with the King
If you accepted Jesus' salvation
and the eternal life with Him that it brings

WE ONLY PASS THIS WAY BUT ONCE

Ecclesiastes 12:7 Then shall the dust return to the earth as it was:
and the spirit shall return unto God who gave it.

She only passed this way but once
still she left her mark for all to see
No matter what she did she did it
with all her heart and with dignity
For she was a proud woman who was
always consistent as she gave her best
Even when the trials of suffering and pains
put her through some devastating test

She was a strong woman and had dignity
that comes only when one is sorely tried
With her head held high and shoulders back
she has shown others her strength and pride
In that no matter the test that in this life
must to each of us surely come
We will all one day come to the end of it
when our race has finally been run

Then only the memories that you
leave to others will prevail
So do your very best and in the end
all your deeds will for you tell
If you passed this way and left a smile
and some joy that will keep your memory alive
Then others will use you as a role model and your
memory like hers will survive

Will someone give you some flowers as
we give to your loved one this day
For she gave to us memories that speak
to us even on this day and say
Give all that you have to give for you
only once pass this way
And the Lord is standing by
to give you your reward
If you lived a life for Him then
no trial for you is too hard

And we all have this appointment
with death that we cannot cancel
For all flesh must return unto its source
and every tongue will tell
If you know the Lord Jesus
as your Redeemer for we cannot hide
My advice is to get to know Him while
you have a choice and live on life's side

IF ONLY I COULD

Ecclesiastes 3:1,2a To everything there is a season, and a time to
every purpose under the heaven: A time to be born, and a time to
die;

If I could I would hold your hand just once more
I would look into your eyes before
you stepped out of the door
If only I could I would give all
the stars in heaven as your due
And I would stand before all
to protect you my whole life through

I would take the time to smell the flowers
and I would give you some too
If only I could I would give the world
and all the good things in it to you
I would take the long way home as
I walked you through the park
I would whisper words to you filled
with love that comes from my heart

If I could I would take away all life's
pains and heartaches
But then how would we learn
from all life's mistakes
How would we grow with the
wisdom needed to run in life's race
And meet the trials and heartaches
that we will all have to face

Death is one thing we can all
be assured to one day see
It is no respecter of person
and it may choose you or me
So today while we all have a chance
to make our own burial plan
Take out some soul insurance and choose
Jesus while you live in this land
For we will all face the trial of death and
one day before a righteous God stand

48

IF I COULD CALL BACK YOUR YESTERDAY

II Peter 3:10a But the day of the Lord will come as a thief
in the night;

If only I had the power to bring back your yesterdays
Then I would take the time and to you say
All the things that you my friend meant to me
I would surely take our friendship more seriously
If yesterday could only be for us a brand new start
I would walk slower and take time
to listen to you with my heart
For in our friendship all of us in the hood do know
That we shared a brotherhood and now we will miss
you so

If I could I would take you safely in my arms
I would protect you from all of life's harms
If only I could I would say my friend
let's walk and not through the hood run
We need to take our time so that we can
smile as on our faces we feel the sun
Let's take our time to really listen and hear
what the birds and bees say
For only once in our lifetime
will we pass this way

But dear friend if I could I would give
more thought to our actions each day
I would try to help lead guide and
show you to a better way
If I could I would to God on your
behalf fall on my knees and pray
Lord please forgive my friend and
give him another day

But dear friend I know that there is nothing I can say
So I will have to learn to for myself pray
That God will have mercy for us
left behind in the hood
That we will take this tragedy and
turn our lives over to do good

I know we only pass this way but once
and we must make our mark then
For no one has the power to call back
yesterday and then begin again
But God is waiting for us to listen
to the call He is sending to all of you
Trust in Him and call on the name of Jesus
and He will of this trial take you through

A LOOK INTO THE THRONE ROOM
Revelation 22:20 He which testifieth these things saith, Surely I
come. Amen. Even so, come, Lord Jesus.

If God would open a small window
in heaven for you to see
And stop time as He gives unto you
a wonderful gift of reprieve
So you could see all the wonderful
pleasures and honor He has given unto me
For I now have a body beautiful without
disease and it's of pain forever free

I would pray that He grant unto you
the eyes that could behold the throne
Then you would be able to see your
darling daughter and she is not alone
For she is with other heavenly beings
that are in the place where they belong
Waiting to start the great celebration
when you and all the other saints get home

Listen and you will surely hear her voice
raised to sing praises loud and clear
With such joy for she is in the place
where the Lamb of God is so near
Can you not see the honor given unto her
as with joy bells ringing she sings
Glory Glory Alleluia to God in the highest
and to Jesus our Saviour and King

NOW I LAY ME DOWN TO SLEEP

Proverbs 3:24 When thou liest down, thou shalt not be afraid: yea,
thou shalt lie down, and thy sleep shall be sweet.

Now when I lay me down
for the last time to sleep
And awake in the morning in
my Master's arms so sweet
For He has promised me that
my soul He would keep
And present me with exceeding joy
with all His other sheep

As I am now privileged to have the joy
of just hanging around the throne
Waiting to start that great celebration when
you and all the other saints get home
Crying is Ok for I know the pain of
separation you must all at this time feel
But death is an intricate part of life
and that never changing fact is so real

But when you have the word of God
as an anchor on which you can stand
No matter the trials and pain we
all endure while living in this sin sick land
For I know of assuredly it's so true
that death has no sting or power over you
When you accept Jesus as your Saviour
then of the grave you're only passing through

On that glorious road that leads to
the mansion designed in the promise land
Where every day will be a Sabbath day
for before the Lord you will forever stand
In the presence of God because you chose
Jesus while the blood in your body was warm
Now the Lord Himself will welcome you home
and you will forever be safe in His loving arms

GIFTS FROM HEAVEN

James 1:17a Every good and perfect gift is from above, and
cometh down from the Father of lights

We your friends and church family Come to support
and celebrate with you and your entire family The
home going of your child, even when we know that
God never makes any mistakes the loss of a child
causes such pain and questioning.

But in His wise provision of seeing what we cannot
see, He has taken your dear little one into His bosom
and now the is just walking around the throne room
waiting to start that great celebration when you and all
the other saints get home

God knows the sorrow that death brings especially
with a child for we never expect to have them have to
leave before us. But remember the Lord said suffer the
little children to come unto me and forbid them not,
Matthew 19:14. God called this special child home
but He allowed you the privilege of enjoying him for a
short time.

Now you can rest in the knowledge that your little one
is free from the snare of this old sinful world and is
waiting for you on yonder shores. When God will
reunite all of His children as we gather together in that
place where there will be no more separations, no
more pain or heartaches and no more tears or good
byes. In that heaven place where we together with our
little one will see our Saviour face to face.

OUR HEAVENLY GIFT
Isaiah 11:6c…and a little child shall lead them.

On that wonderful day God allowed
a precious son to be given unto us
He was so special that God Himself
wanted our baby son to rush
Back into the throne room for even
though with us he has a special place
The Lord wanted our son by His side so
He would by His own amazing grace
Save our baby boy so he would be assured
of seeing the Lord face to face

We love you son and in our heart there
is a place reserved just for you there
Even though the heartache is almost
too heavy for loving parents to bear
We thank God for the privilege
of holding him in our arms and to share
Together this precious baby boy who
has drawn us closer to each other as we
Mourn our loss we thank you Father
for allowing our son to return unto Thee

RETURNED TO THE SENDER

James 1:17a Every good gift and every perfect gift is from
above, and cometh down from the Father of light.

Little grandson you were not with us for long
For God wanted you to hurry back to His throne
Now we will no longer see your sweet smile
Because you were with us only for a short while

Your new tooth I also will not be able to see
For you will show it to God now instead of me
Instead of taking your first steps
you now fly on angel's wings
And are blessed to glorify God
as you lift your sweet little voice to sing

We will all miss you so much and
we will often think of you and cry
Many a day will pass and in our
minds we ask the question Lord why
We know Lord that You understand
and are in absolute control
And our darling little angel child
is in your arms for You to now hold

But God we still are hurting so
bad and don't really understand
We know that You feel our pain
because you too were tested as a man
Give us Lord we pray Your strength to
hold us up under this burden we feel today
Help us to praise You and give You thanks
for sending this special child our way

Now the gift has been returned
to the sender with great love
For we know that this precious gift
came from the Lord above
One that was loved cherished enjoyed
and held in our hearts so near
So forgive us when we lose our composure
for we just have to shed some tears

We thank God for this precious gift
for you made life richer to me
And I know that we have to let go
for your spirit is now completely free
To soar into that great beyond as God
Himself takes you by your little hand
See you on the morrow sweet baby boy
when we too will meet you in that eternal land

Angel Child

Luke 18:16 But Jesus called them unto him, and said, Suffer little children to come unto me, and forbid them not: for of such is the kingdom of God.

Sent from heaven for just a little while
This angel child sent to us and caused
our days to be full of smiles
She has to returned to heaven and
now will on the clouds play
She is so happy because she is with
her heavenly Father today

And she has a beautiful smile
on her little radiant face
As she swings on the pearly gates
in that heavenly place
She can now lift up her voice to
Almighty God as she bows her head in praise
For the Lamb of God is near and she is
surrounded by His amazing grace

Those of us who were privileged to hold
you even for only a few days
Thank our heavenly Father that
He chose to send you our way
The very essence of you and the joy of
having such a beautiful child
Will leave us such wonderful memories
as you leave us only for a short while

Love You Always

SLEEP LITTLE ONE THE ANGELS ARE WATCHING

Matthew 18: 10b That in heaven their angels do always behold
the face of my Father which is in heaven.

Close your eyes and sleep
on my precious little one
Go on and take your rest
for your race has been run
The hand that I wanted to hold
and through life guide
Has left for my sweet little on
e is now resting at my Master's side

When I have cried until the
my heart almost consumes
All of me and I am completely filled
with nothing but agony and gloom
The arms that once held you so near
with your warmth filling all of me
Are now empty and there is nothing
to fill the place where you alone should be

My eyes are so full of all the things
that were picked especially for you
Now they too have no place here
for they only cause me to be so blue
My sweet child I know that somehow
I must find the strength to go on
But it's so hard to believe that you
are now gone and I feel so all alone

I will look to the hills from which
cometh my help O' Lord please
Hear my moans and lift my head up
high above this pain I wait on Thee
For I know You will deliver and
give me peace as I accept Thy will
And I know that You will carry me through
this suffering trial if I just be still

Lord I know not why this tragedy
had to my sweet little one come
But I will still trust You with them
because You are the One
Who always watches over us from
the cradle to the grave
And I know that my darling baby
is surely now from the evil one saved

HEART'S DESIRE

Deuteronomy 4:29 But if from thence thou shalt seek the Lord
thy God, thou shalt find him, if thou seek him with all thy heart
and with all thy soul.

He came and made a difference
in all our lives as you can see
He was a wonderful father figure
and a role model he learned to be
Gave of himself with a love so strong
that even he did not fully know
The rewards and honor that on him
others would on this day bestow

For as a role model he had to walk
a narrow road for you see
He had to always remember that
his steps would have to one day fit me
He tried for me to stay but God
had said of this life you must leave
No flesh and blood will enter into my rest
and be from pain and suffering free

So come unto Me but first the corrupt must
put on the incorruptible to sit at table
For as the Good Shepherd I promised you
My yoke is easy so rest now from your labor
Come Oh seeker and you will find the mansion
for you He promised for it is now prepared
For you may now enter into that glorious place
prepared just for you as one of God heirs

Because while the blood in you was warm
you accepted the Lord Jesus you can share
In the promise of eternal life with Him
and rest in His tender loving care
As the angels in heaven sing to the glory
of God and praises to He who sits on the throne
So I will see you on the morrow when I too
finally finish my race and also come on home

LORD WE NEED THEE

Psalm 46:1GOD is our refuge and strength, a very present
help in trouble.

Lord this pain and heartache is
almost too much for us to bear
Please God we need You to of this
burden and tragedy with us share
For You alone know that we are so hurt
for we have lost our brother
It's hard to understand how men can
do such devastating things to each other

God we need You as never before
for only You Lord understand
The pain of the ones left when
their loved one is taken out of this land
Yes another young black man has
been cheated out of his life
Lord we ask please help us live
in the hood without all of this strife

This pain that is continually surrounding
us can only be lifted by Your grace
For the loss of a loved one leaves
a void that cannot in this life be replaced
And we will always remember our brother
though we will never again see his face
No one else will ever be able to fill the
void in our hearts for this was his place

The memories that we once shared will
stay forever in our hearts and our minds
Our times shared will never be forgotten
for the love we had will forever us bind

As this family will pull together and we will
keep his memories forever alive everyday
We'll remember the good times and we will
surely cry for to you we can no longer say

Dear brother we will miss you wished the Lord
would have allowed you a little longer to stay
But we entrust you to God for He said vengeance
is mine and for all the sins of men I will repay
So dearly loved ones remember that one
day we will all have to leave this old land
I just want to admonish each of you
to accept Jesus as Saviour and take a stand

Because death is a promise given to
each and every one for God's word is true
And the dust must return unto the earth
from which it came no matter what we do
This it is not the end and we will all
one day have to meet God face to face
But for now He alone can lift you up out
of this grieving sorrowful place

And death will no longer have any victory
over us nor the grave have any sting
When we become children of God we
inherit all the promises that this brings
So when old death for us comes around
we will lift our voices and with joy sing
Glory Glory Halleluiah we are going
to spend eternity with our Saviour and King

SOMETIMES EVEN THE STRONG HAVE TO CRY

II Corinthians 12:9 And he said unto me, My grace is sufficient
for my strength is made perfect in weakness.

Sometimes even the strongest of us have to cry
The burdens get too heavy
for us so we ask God why
Why Lord is all this heartache
and pain given in the life of men
No matter where we turn or what
we do it seems we can never win

Death has once again shown up
in our lives even at the front gate
Moved into our midst to cause so much
pain is this always to be our fate
God where are You we prayed
Lord please don't take our loved one from us
Put all our faith in You prayed day and night
but it seemed not to be enough

I thought when we beseeched the Father
that we would surely in this matter prevail
We prayed so we thought he would not
at this time have to go down death's trail
But even though all power in heaven and
earth even death is in His mighty hand
Death is one thing that because of sin
will come upon each and every man

But the Lord has told us to fret not death
for if we believe in Him who conquered all
Then will we trust in our Maker who knows
what we need and will not suffer us to fall

When we lean and depend on Jesus then
we turn all that pertaineth unto us over to Him
For we know that our loved one can rest in His
tender loving arms so we release them

As we ourselves make preparations
in this life to follow Jesus and live for the Lord
We will hope in His word that we will see our loved
one again so his death will not be so hard
For it is appointed unto man once to die but
the Lord Himself has paved for us the way
He said I Am the way the truth and the life
and when we trust in Him then one day

We will all meet in the throne room and
testify of how we made it over in time
As we stand in the presence of the Lord
as He declares that these souls are mine
Then our robes will be washed in His
blood and be glistening as white as snow
As we will spend eternity together
praising the Lord for then we will all know

The glory of a new life with Him in that
eternal land where we will with Him stand
And be His children all because we gave
Him our lives while we lived in this land
It's Ok to shed a few tears for I know
you will miss seeing my smiling face
Just remember that I am with my Saviour
and be happy for His amazing grace
That will usher me into the throne room
where I will find my prepared place

IT'S ALL IN THE PLAN

Psalm 30:5b weeping may endure for a night, but joy cometh in
the morning.

Lord it's so hard to say
Goodbye to those we love
Sweet Jesus help us and
send your strength from above
Keep Lord we pray your
loving arm around us today
Show your mercy to those left
behind help us find the way

When death comes around and
causes so much pain and our lives disrupt
Then we call on Thee most
Holy God and in You put our trust
Yesterday is gone sweet Jesus and
tomorrow may never be mine
So teach us Lord to number our days
and to give You some of our time

For only once can we in this old world
make a difference to those around
So we can leave a heritage of love
for our family that will abound
But even with this heritage of love we still
all need to take the time so we can see
That death is something that none of us can
avoid and it may choose you or me

So while it is called today we should take the
time and choose Jesus so He can set us free
And have His blessed assurance that with
Him we will have the right to spend eternity
For God so loved the world that He suffered
and died and made a way that we may be saved
As it is in His plan that on our pathway to glory
we will all have to pass through the grave

HE GAVE ME SPACE

II Peter 3:9 The Lord is not slack concerning his promises, as
some men count slackness; but is longsuffering to us-ward, not
willing that any should perish, but that all should come to
repentance.

Thank God this trial of suffering and pain
is over and He gave me space
Through it all He allowed me to know Him
before I had to meet Him face to face
Oh I know many will remember all
the old things in my life they have seen
But when I asked for forgiveness He called
me unto Himself and wiped my slate clean

Many are the good memories shared
with loved ones so you will surely cry
Asking ourselves the same question
that others have asked in times gone by
But believe me He knew what was best
for me so when He took my hand
In the sweet hour of my departure I had
His assurance on which I could stand

For He said all that labor and are
heavy-laden can come unto to me
Jesus paid for all my sins when He shed
His blood for all sinners on Calvary
In His mercy He allowed me the privilege
in this sickness to call on His great name
Weeping may endure for a night but joy
cometh when He washes away sin's shame

Cry a little as you think of me but don't forget
what God has in His great mercy done for me
This frail body you see is only the old house where I
used to live for my spirit is now soaring so free
So Goodbye to one and all it's been so sweet being
with you but now I must answer my Master's call
I admonish you to remember that death is an intricate
part of life and it will visit you one and all

But the sting has been taken out of death
and the victory removed from the grave
When the blood in your body is warm you accept
Jesus Christ as Saviour then you too can be saved
Though now you are sad for you will no longer hear
my voice or look upon my smiling face anymore
Smile when you think of me and our times together
remember that although I have stepped onto eternity shore
I am now completely free and I am waiting for you as
you pass through the grave to heaven's welcoming
door

We your friends come to support and uplift you in
this your time of need. It is so hard to say goodbye
to loved ones especially those who shared our
formative years along with our hardships and our triumphs.
One who teased yet protected us as only a brother can.
The love we share with a sibling is so unique and
can never be duplicated No matter the different kinds
of love relationships we have in our lives So we who
have had the pleasure of knowing the love of a sister
or brother are counted as blessed

God knows all about the pain you feel even though others
only see your smiling face Remember His promise to one
day wipe them all away, **Revelation 21:4** But until then
you have an anchor to which you can lean on and praise
be to God, He has also given unto you a church family
that loves you and are standing just a whisper away
waiting for your call

Believe me if the Lord delay His coming we will be
there, if only to lend a shoulder for you to lean on or a
hand to hold even a listening ear to hear and to pray for
and with you. While we cannot take away your pain at
the loss of you brother we can through empathy share it
with you

I'LL FLY AWAY

Job 14:14a If a man die, shall he live again?

Our lives are but a vapor that stays
around only for a short while
But what we do can leave good
memories of a kind and gentle smile
Because we know the appointment
that was before his birth made
God said death will come to one and
all and cannot be cancelled in anyway

He was here a short time and we thought we
had many more years he looked forward to
But when the Lord calls the spirit your time
on this old sinful earth is through
No matter that you did not have the time
to say goodbye or give a hug or a final smile
Nor did you sit down for a last visit or just hang
around with loved ones for a little while

God knows what the future ha
in store for each and every man
He admonished us to lay up our treasures
in heaven for this is His plan
And as surely as a man must die He will
one day be raised and live again
No one knows when death will come but
we can have the victory over death and win

If while the breath of life is in your body
you made the right choice
For you will have to choose now
for pass the grave you will have no voice
So when death steals a loved one though
we feel the pain of this loss have no doubt
We know that Jesus came and conquered
death no matter how death came about

The Lord watches over the affairs of men
to bring us to an expected end
He watches and He hears our cries and
feels our sorrows because He is our truest friend
Yes we will miss our loved one but God loves him
and made a way for him to have space
So when he lives again he will be so happy
for he has a chance to see our Saviour face to face

SWEET FLOWER IS GONE ON HOME

I Corinthians 15:53 For this corruptible must put on incorruption,
and this mortal must put on immortality.

God sent a flower that was born
lived and nurtured in the hood
He had a mindset to do better
and he wanted to for others do good
Then one day this little flower heard
the sweet sound of music in his ear
And thought I will give words to
this sound so that others in the hood can hear

For they needed something to give meaning
to their lives that they hold so dear
So the music became a charge that uplifted
his heart and gave new life for others to hear
He searched for the sweet worlds to put
in a form to make them sound just right
Words that could reach out to others and
give them directions in the darkness of night

For you see God used this little ghetto flower
to reach many in their darkest hour
For it was surely His hand that formed
the plan to place this sweet little flower
In our midst to give us such joy and happiness
and show to us such a unique kind of love
As he touched all those who he came in contact
with for you see he was sent from above

Now even though our hearts are very sad
and the tears we shed are there for all to see
How much this little flower has touched us
and was loved by everyone especially by me
But I know although he seemed so very young
his course had been finished and his race run
For I realize that just the other night he received
the summons that came only from the Son

And he knew that although his loved ones
would be sorrowful he had to obey
For from the very beginning God is
over all life and He has the final say
As just the other night the street lights come on
and knew it was time for you to hurry home
So dear one we will truly miss you but know
that you had to answer this summons alone
For God had given you an appointment
that you couldn't cancel because it came directly
from the throne

But the good news for us on this very sad day
Is if we call on the name of Jesus and
let Him have His way
He will make intercession for us
and our sins His blood will cover
If we lean on Him we will receive
the comfort that can come from no other

LOVE IN ACTION

I Thessalonians 1:3 Remembering without ceasing your work of
faith, and labour of love, and patience of hope in our Lord Jesus
Christ, in the sight of God and our Father;

When I look at all the things that you do
To uplift others to help them get through
Then I know that God is working through you
To show His amazing kind of grace filled with love
That only comes from our Heavenly Father above

So I just want to take the time and thank you too
And say by your kindness you
kept me from being so blue
Thanks for letting the Lord use you
to be to me so kind
For I know it was only Him
that kept me and my family on your mind

I wish that for us you always remember to pray
For it is only by His strength
can we with this burden stay
As we know that in all things
We must give Him the glory
For in the end only what we do
for Christ will tell the real gospel story

And when the trials of life weigh us down as to us they come as we know they will. Then the Father will send a loving hand to support us when the tears will not be stilled. For the pains and heartaches that come when we lose a loved one are so fresh in our minds then we must lean on Jesus for His strength for He will not allow sorrow to us forever bind. And we have His blessed assurance that even in the death of a loved one no one who accepts His blood atonement will be left behind

When death that old enemy shows up we can be assured, that Jesus has conquered him and is standing by to strengthen you. He promised he would not leave you comfortless, **Jn. 14:18.** Remember He is the ultimate promise keeper and heaven and earth shall pass away before one title or dot of His Word shall fail.

He will not leave you in this your time of suffering. Just call and He will answer, He is a present help in your time of trouble, **Ps. 46:1**. Lean on His and He will carry you through.

We are praying for and with you, call and we will answer.

A KIND TOUCH

I John 4:7a Beloved, let us love one another: for love is of
God;

Thank you so much for your kind sweet touch
That in my time of sorrow meant to me so much
Thank you for your gift that to me was so kind
I know that it was God who put me on your mind

So to Him I will give for your kindness all the glory
And pray He remembers you
for this at the end of your life's story
For He said I will for all your
goodness to my children repay
I see all and will give you a
good reward one glorious day

So for now with the few little words I know
I just want to thank you again for your kindness shows
For we all one day will have to through many trials go
But together the burden is not too hard to bear
As long as we have others to show that for us they
care

NO CHANCE FOR CANCELLATION

Hebrews 9:27 And as it is appointed unto men once to die, but
after this the judgment:

Death is an intricate part of life and
this never changing fact is so real
No matter who death calls be it sister
father brother or mother there is no appeal
So I will testify that life is only the beginning
on our journey to death and that's the real deal
When a man is born he is granted only a few years
to live on this old sinful earth wherein he plods
But he is given the heart and free will to accept
the gift of atonement that comes only from God

Death is the way we all must go and we will
spend eternity somewhere please don't doubt this
For He said that the dust must return to the earth
as it was and the spirit to He who gave it
Mother has gone but the sweet memories
of her life and those she touched will forever last
Remember with joy the things she did to make your
life brighter and one day this heartache will pass
Weeping may endure for a night but you can just lean
on God and He will take you through this task

Looking back at all the good times and the hardships
too we can see a void is left that cannot be filled
Sometimes in our sorrow the tears seem to have a will
of their own and they just refuse to dry up or keep still
In our somber moments when all is quiet we seem to
hear her voice saying it's Ok for this is the Father's
will

Mother lived loved and touched many people as she
passed through on her way to the great beyond in eternity
Just look around and you will see the love that is shown
to her family by friends as their support we came to be

I want to remind you that Jesus said all who labor and are
heavy-laden come unto Me and I will give them rest
Mother just the other day heard the call of the Master
and decided that for her He knew what was best
For God had promised all who hear His voice that if we
heed His call then we could be for all eternity saved
Then death can have no victory for God so loved us that
He conquered death when His only begotten Son He gave
By Jesus' sacrifice we understand when we accept His
free gift then on our pathway to glory we must pass
through the grave

I'LL CRY TOMORROW

Psalm 107:19 Then they cry unto the Lord in their trouble,
and he saveth them out of their distresses.

I'll cry tomorrow although today
I am in such pain and am so sad
Tomorrow is the day I'll cry
remembering this great loss I've had
Remembering mother when I call
our name and it hits that you are not there
When I just want to hear your voice and
tell you of things we used to share

Tomorrow when I'll be alone and wonder
how to go on praying this pain will pass
Then the tears will flow as if a well has
opened in my heart that will forever last
When my heart is overwhelmed I'll cry
tomorrow for the one who yesterday went away
You stepped into eternity into the arms of God and
there was nothing we could do or say

But I thank God for the sweet
sweet memories to each of us you gave
Memories that say we can make it
even through the pain of losing you today
Yes although death is an intricate part of life
it still leaves us with a great void
And going on without you in our lives
mother is really going to be very hard

But with the help of God I'll save my tears
until tomorrow and celebrate today
For you had a life well spent and
you lived it to the fullest in every way
Left us a heritage that many will envy
for you were a great role model as a mother
And I will not cry today because I want this great
celebration to be like no other

So I will dear mother just ask God to welcome
you into His presence in that eternal land
For you have now passed beyond all that man
can do for you and you are now in God's hands
And He promised that if while the blood runs warm
in our body we accept Him for all to see
Then from the sting of death and the victory
over the grave is what He promised to you and me

AND THEN CAME THE BEGINNING

Ecclesiastes 12:7 Then shall the dust return to the earth as it was:
and the spirit shall return unto God who gave it.

Man was born to live for a short time
but he also was born to die
When our loved ones pass over
to the other side we often wonder why
Lord I just don't always understand
he was too young to have to leave this land
Death stole him without giving us a chance
to say goodbye it took him out of our hand

Now the memories that we shared over
the years will have to last us a lifetime
For he took a stroll into eternity
the other day and had to leave us all behind
You see the day he was born he had
an appointment with death that he had to keep
Now don't get me wrong he lived his life
to the fullest and to him it was oh so sweet

He made many good friends and had loved
ones that really cared and treasured him
He left some sweet some happy and some sad
memories to each and every one of them
He walked this old earth for his appointed
life's span until just the other day
When his spirit heard the sound of the Master's
call and it had to listen to what God had to say

As the Father called unto your loved one's
inner man that his new beginning was on the way
Come unto me all that labor and are heavy-laden
and I will give you rest from your labor today

So when he lay down for the last time in this
old sinful world to take his rest and sleep
His inner man recognized when next he woke
it would be in that eternal land and with God he
would have to meet

So dear loved ones family and friends remember
it is appointed unto every man once to die
You will have to meet with the Lord whether it's in
death through the grave or in the rapture in the sky
So today as we came to say our last goodbye to our
friend and loved one Just keep this fact in mind
Jesus paid the price for our sins so that even in death
from Him we do not have to be left behind

Oh death where is your victory oh grave
where is your sting you lost your power
when salvation Jesus did bring
The only way back to the Father after
we pass from life is to go through
the grave on our way to see the King
Knowing that we must pass from mortality
into our new beginning to get to the
mansion God has prepared for us
So before death calls and takes a hold
on you please accept the blood atonement
of Jesus and in Him put your trust

FROM THE HEART OF A DEVOTED WIFE

Proverbs 14:1 Every wise woman buildeth her house: but the
foolish plucketh it down with her hands.

Maybe you didn't see in my spouse what I saw
Maybe you don't understand how I feel at my loss
Maybe he has really gone to a better place where he is
no longer in pain that plagues the human race

Maybe my memories of this
loss will in time start to fade
But I will always cherish the
memories that together we made
And the pain will lessen and
life will to me become more kind
Maybe the sun without his smiling face
will again for me shine

I know that whatever happens
in the future my eyes cannot see
So I want to say thank you Lord
for giving my husband unto me
I pray that as he came into my life
to brighten my days
That I was also a comfort to him
in my own small way

Missing him will now just be
a part of my everyday life
But I thank God for him
as he made my life so bright
So when the tears of sorrow overtake
me in the middle of the night
I will just remember our time together as I hold on
until the day light

Goodbye for now dear loved one
your time on this earth is through
And given a choice you would
not come back and that's the whole truth
So those standing in this place
I admonished each and every one of you
It's time to get right with God for one day
death will come for you too

HE GIVETH HIS BELOVED REST

Revelation 14:13 And I heard a voice from heaven saying unto
me, Write, Blessed are the dead which die in the Lord from
henceforth: Yea, saith the Spirit, that they may rest from their
labour and their works do follow them.

Praise the Lord Alleluia Thank
You Jesus I am finally free
When you look at this old frail body
remember it's really not me
God has been so good and He has
given unto me a wonderful life
When I look back on my blessings
even when there was sickness and strife

Counting up the years as they just
seemed to take wings and fly
He blessed me with over 90 years
and sometimes I had to wondered why
Why the Lord left me behind when others
just seem to fade away
Old death had no dominion over me
until God allowed it just the other day

Look at all my loved ones my heritage
both young and old that stood in the gap for me
Showing love in action as they earnestly prayed
that from my suffering I would be set free
Please hold on to that love I shared with each of you
and let it radiate towards others for all to see
For there is no greater plan from God than this
that your love grows and becomes as strong as a tree

Listen and maybe God will allow you
to hear as hark the herald angels do sing
Blow the trumpet lift the voices on high
for into the throne room another saint they do bring
She has fought a good fight and has finished her
course and she can now from her labor rest
For God gave her a charge that she kept
for over 90 years and now at last comes the best

With Him as her anchor death would have
no fear for God had taken the victory from the grave
She would want all her loved ones to accept
Jesus as Saviour so they too would be saved
For in her years of sojourning on this old land she
found out that Jesus was waiting to take her hand
So if you want to see her again in the glory of the Lord
then you too must all make a decision while
you yet live in this old sinful land

GOD KNOWS

Hebrews 4:15 For we have not an high priest which cannot be
touched with the feeling of our infirmities; but was in all points
tempted like as we are, yet without sin.

Sometimes when words will not comfort
or relieve the pain in our hearts
When we hurt so bad that we feel like
these gushing tears will never depart
We hear words of sympathy but
don't understand just what they mean
We walk around in a daze thinking
this is not real it's surely a dream

It's too hard Dear Lord to think
I will never see my son again
To imagine that in this life the pain
of losing him will never end
Even though we know that death is an intricate
part of life and it's always around the bend
We can never prepare for the devastating pain
when old death seems to always win

In this time of such heart rendering grief
there is only One who understands your great loss
God knows the pain you are going through for His Son
too died when He was crucified on the cross
But thank your Heavenly Father for the pain and
heartache Jesus suffered as He was tested the same as us
He is our comforter standing at the right hand of the
Father making intercession and in Him we can trust

In this time of such great pain we can lean on
Jesus and let Him our heavy burdens bear
He is our strong tower and a present help in this time
of grief and He will of our heartaches and pains share
For He gave us the right to come boldly before His
throne whereby we might receive His mercy
And He promised if we accept His blood atonement
He would take from the grave death's sting and
give us the victory

THE CRY OF A WOUNDED HEART

Psalm 34:6 This poor man cried, and the LORD heard him, and
saved him out of all his troubles.

We know that the signs of the times are fast
pointing to the day of Your return it seems
For men are becoming so fierce but
You promised that on You we could always lean
Lord teach us the wisdom of Your ways so that in
times like these we will seek You and pray
For the pain of death came and snatched
little Mike out of our midst just the other day

And we are so heartbroken and the tears just seem to
be gushing out of eyes that need Thee
As the adversary meant this for bad but You said
suffer the little Children to come unto me
We know not the reason for this tragedy but God's
promises are all true and He allowed this to be
We know not why a child is taken but
he is taken from the evil to come so blessed is he

Lord hear our cries and deliver us
from this agonizing pain for death has once again
Come into our midst and this time snuffed
out a young life that had really just began
The pains of these circumstances are so hard
for us to understand and try to bear
So dear Jesus we come laying our heavy
burden at Your feet for we know You care

We come to Thee Father because You
said cast all your care on Me for I care for you
Father this pain of losing little Mike
is too heavy so we need You to carry us through
Give us a forgiving heart as we stand before You
we ourselves may receive forgiveness too
Stand by us Lord uphold in Your strength
and tempter us in all that we say or do

Remind us that every man must the grave
pass through to get to that Promised Land
Give us a clean heart so we store up good
memories of little Mike for his life is out of our hands
Jesus that perfect Lamb of God is near and promised
we could call on Him in our time of trouble
Only He has the power to deliver us from this
suffering and the agony of this tragedy like no other

Hold fast to the faith that is within you for His
strength is made perfect in our weakness
And Jesus will uphold you throughout
this trial and in the midst of it give you rest
Then on the morrow when God gathers us
with little Mike at His great white throne
If while the blood is warm in your body you
accepted Jesus He will also welcome you home

THE SAFE WAY OUT

Jeremiah 9:20a 21 Yet hear the word of the LORD, O ye women,
21For death is come up into our windows, and is entered into our
palaces, to cut off the children from without, and the young men
from the streets.

Oh Lord will this agony of death with
this pain and heartache never end
Yesterday old death came and stole
my son who was also my friend
How long oh Lord will our young men
continue to kill each other
Do they not know that we come from the same
ancestral seed and they are brothers

Look into the eyes of those who are left
now to mourn and cry especially his mother
Do our young black brothers not know that
for these sins of destruction there is no cover
Can we Lord as a people continue to prosper when
our young men are killing each other in the streets
So Lord we mothers come with bowed heads and
weep with our pain and lay this burden at Your feet

Father change the minds and hearts of our young
people so that they may seek You while You are near
Teach them to come to You so that even when old
death comes around we will have no reason to fear
For we know that if it is in this world only
we have hope then our lives are already in defeat
But if while the blood is warm in our body we choose
Jesus then at the foot of the cross we will find peace

The Lord said in His holy word that
vengeance is mine and He will repay
Young black brothers seek God while you
still have time and He will lead you in the right way
And if you choose Jesus you will find that death
is the door through the grave to heaven's pathway
Jesus took the victory from the grave and the way
to heaven He has by His blood for you paved
So none be lost the way for you is now opened
if you accept His blood atonement you can be saved

If while the blood runs warm in your body and the
breathe is still in you and you make the right choice
You must choose now for when death comes around
you will no longer in the decision have a voice
God so loves you that He would have you live in this
old sinful world and to be sin free
So dear brothers surrender your lives to He who will
set you at liberty for He has already paid for
your sins when He died on that cursed tree

HE IS OUR PRESENT HELP

Psalm 34: 19 Many are the afflictions of the righteous: but the
LORD delivereth him out of them all.

Sometimes when words seem too small
to comfort and tears just won't cleanse
Then is the time to lean on Jesus
who really is our most faithful friend
Sometimes when the way seems so dark
and lonely and tears our only companion
God waits for you to call on Him and He
will carry you through for He is our champion

He will share your burdens and
strengthen you as no other can do
God told us that we can cast all our
cares on Him for He careth for you
No matter how big the problems He knows
that there is nothing really new
For remember just like a man He
was tested on all points too

He understands all our heartaches and
our burdens He promised to share
If we would only lean on Him as we
bring them to Him in prayer
Weeping is the natural thing to do
when a loved one steps out into eternity
For I am only looking at the presences
and thinking of those left like me

And we really do know that a place
in eternity is promised to every man
But you have the choice to make
while you live in this old sinful land
For you must make your own
Reservation it's all in your hands
To choose Jesus for God's justice
must be paid on demand

Choose you this day to serve God
and be assured of the right kind of pay
For the Lord's Word is true and to kneel
before death one day we will all lay
God through His Son has revealed to every
woman and man the beautiful salvation plan
I beseech thee to take a stand so you will be
assured of getting to the Promised Land

Then how beautiful this place you will
see as we with Him live in eternity
A mansion in heaven not made
by hands He has promised to thee
If I would just give Him my life
while the breath is still in me
I can be clothed in His glory that
He has prepared when he set me free

One day it's been promised to every man
that before a righteous God we must all stand
In His righteousness or alone and defenseless
without His love it's all in your hand
If you will stand victorious in His glory
and covered by His precious saving blood
Able to face Almighty God as Jesus has already
covered us by His grace and mighty love

All because on that day you exercised
the free will that was given unto thee
And you used it so wisely after He revealed
Himself and as a faithful one you came to be
The owner of a mansion in heaven that He
has prepared just for you and me
When He took all of our sins and nailed them
to that old rugged cross way out on Calvary

May God bless you and comfort you is my prayer

THE FINAL CURTAIN CALL

Revelation 14:13b...Blessed are the dead which die in the lord
from henceforth: Yea, saith the Spirit, that they may rest from
their labours; and their works do follow them.

When my life is over on this side of the curtain
And you see my physical body no more
Then lift up your eyes to God for He knows
That I have only moved to yonder shores

When my head is laid down for the last time
Just remember that I had joy because Jesus was mine
How beautiful is the knowledge of
the new life I am going to live
All because while I still had breath
in my body my life to Jesus I did give

Precious are those that die in the Lord
for to live for Him brings great rewards you see
He will not suffer you to be separated even through
the trials of life that come upon thee
For He said in His Word I go away to prepare a
mansion in heaven for you that He created
Absent from the body present with Him is His promise
given to every sanctified tongue and nation

If you follow Jesus for He is The Way
The Truth and The Light so you will be prepared
When He comes back again and meets
with His saints either in death or in the air
Jesus is the faithful promise keeper and
we have the promise to us He made
That we could live with Him in our mansion in
eternity after we pass through the grave

Please accept Jesus while you can choose
while the blood is still warm and the life is in thee
Only He has the power to deliver you
from the adversary and to set you free
The price has already been paid no need
to worry just have faith in this life to see
That only in this world can you
with your volition will choose
To follow Jesus for in Him
you cannot your reward lose

He would that none be lost
remember He paid the price at the cross
This world that I once called home was
just a waiting station to prepare us who were lost
So now dear loved ones please remember
me every now and then with a smile
Give thanks to Almighty God that
He lent me to you for a little while
Then thank Him for allowing you
to travel this road with me as I
finished my course and ran my last mile

THANKS NEVER SEEMS TO BE ENOUGH

II Corinthians 1:3-4 Blessed be God, even the Father of our Lord
Jesus Christ, the Father of mercies, and God of all comfort; 4
who comforteth us in all our tribulation, that we may be able to
comfort them which are in any trouble, by the comfort wherewith
we ourselves are comforted of God.

When I was in need of comfort
I asked God and He sent you
He used your hands to let His
love come pouring through
Yes just an ordinary person who
allowed the Maker free reigns
So that I could feel His love and
know that I am not alone in this pain

We who bring comfort are very blessed
to be used while bringing glory to His name
For even the smallest gifts of comfort
shows the world what they should seek to gain
Even the saints cry sometimes for losing
a loved one can be a devastating thing
We know that the Lord hears us so we hold
you up in prayer for the relief it brings

So with thanksgiving we thank God
for all of you holding us up in prayer to the Lord
With His help using ordinary people we
can make it even if the trials seem very hard
Now we must just gird up the loins of our minds
and testify of your comfort and good deeds
That our heavenly Father hears our cries and
He answers through other people who go to
Him on our behalf and He supplies our every need

WHEN WE DON'T ALWAYS UNDERSTAND
Philippians 1:29 For unto you it is given in the behalf of Christ,
not only to believe on him, but also to suffer for his sake;

Sometimes when we just don't understand
This is the time we must lean on God and not man
And allow Him to take our hand
for He alone knows the complete plan
So He lent our loved one to guide
and to help us so we thank God
For the few years on this old sinful
earth he with us did plod

He is now free because He made
the decision a long time ago
When he decided that following Jesus
was the only way he wanted to go
He fought a good fight finished his race
and stood as long and he could
For the Master made him a mighty warrior
and this assignment he understood

He climbed the highest mountain
and sang a glorious song
He truly witnessed for his Master
all his sanctified life long
He ran a good race and kept the faith
and his course was finally won
While those who are left behind
can only pray God's will be done

You know he loved you and he
really didn't want to leave
But the Master was calling
and Him he wanted to please
He decided just the other day
to go on and accept his pay
Remember he hung around
a long time so we could see
And witness his faith in God
which strengthened you and me

Although the treasure stored
in this earthly tabernacle is no more
You have the blessed assurance
you will meet him on the distant shore
So dry your tears and thank God
for his life because he was ready to go home
Just remember if you too accept Jesus as
Saviour then this parting will not be very long

With the Holy Ghost sent to lead
you through the grave as your guide
All because you chose Jesus you too
will be able to rest at the Master's side
Because without Jesus as you guide
the evil one as an angel will himself disguise
Then you will find that even under the rocks
you cannot from judgment hide

GOD KNOWS

I Corinthians 2:9 But as it is written, Eye hath not seen, nor ear heard, neither have entered into the heart of man, the things which God hath prepared for them that love him.

We family and friends come as a conduit to stand in the gap for you and uphold you as God's strength enfolds and uplift you in this trial of endurance with the loss of your loved one. We empathize with you and call on the wonderful name of Jesus who will comfort you in this your time of need.

Death is an entity that invades all of our lives at one time or another. Yet even though it causes such pain at the void left to those who must endure this heartache, it is God's plan and will come to us one and all. Words will never really express the feelings of those who experience this loss, but we want to remind you that prayer really does change things. So we offer up to Almighty God our heartfelt prayers on your behalf. Remember Earth has no sorrow that heaven cannot heal. Death is the last enemy that the Lord God has put under our feet, for we do not sorrow as those that have no hope. Because it is given unto us to know mystery that the blood atonement has purchased for us.

So even when we lay down for the last time in this old sinful world, although we know that the dust must return unto the earth from which it came and that our spirit will return to the Lord who gave it, Ecclesiastes 12:7, death has no victory over us. This is only the new beginning for your loved one and he awaits for you on yonder shore. For we know if we accept the blood atonement shed for us then when we are absent from the body we are present with the Lord, II Corinthians 5:6.

HERE WE WILL TAKE OUR REST

Revelation 14:13 And I heard a voice from heaven saying unto
me, Write, Blessed are the dead which die in the Lord from
henceforth: Yea, saith the Spirit, that they may rest from their
labours; and their works do follow them.

Jesus wept, and groaned in His Spirit for all to see
He felt the pain and agony of death the same as thee
He was tested on all points so He really does know
The pain of separation that death for you holds

He knew all the pain that death to you would bring
For He also suffered as He too
felt the agony of death's sting
How very dark and dreary the way
for us that are left behind
Sometimes wondering in our sorrow
will peace ever again be mine

Even though we all really expect
for death to come but not to me
Surely with the love we shared
death for us just can't ever be
We just hold on tight and pray
for each other every day
Then maybe God will forget His word
and not send death our way

How Oh Lord can we be expected
to bear this all-consuming pain
We must just lean on Jesus and believe
that we will see our loved one again
For one day not too far away when
we will be able to look to the yonder shore
We will see that death is no more than
stepping out through eternity's door

So if we only could to you now have anything to say
It would be to tell you that you
need God in your life this day
Then you will also be assured that
your mansion for you is prepared
So no matter if you meet Him in death
or if you rise to meet the Master in the air

SISTER WE ARE STILL TO EACH OTHER
SO NEAR
Galatians 6:2 Bear ye one another's burdens, and so fulfill
the law of Christ.

Dear sister although your physical body I cannot see
I know in my heart you have not gone far from me
You have just stepped over on
the other side of the wall
But in my heart you are still near to us all

When you were first born into this old world
You were so special as the first born baby girl
You were the older one so you
had to lead me by my hand
You taught me so much that
I needed in this world to stand

Then dear sister much to my surprise
God ordained that I should to the top rise
To be the one to lead and for you take care
Of all your needs as I was given your burdens to bear

So now when it seems that I am in this world alone
I know that in this place
called time is where I now belong
So with my head held high and
my back straight I will in nowise
Be sorrowful for that time
when we shared each other's lives

But if I could have just one last word to you say
I would thank God that you
were with me until that day
I pray that one day all the
family will in peace of God see
His glory when He calls and
says all who labor come unto me

For Jesus has paid the price
for your ransom out on Calvary
And if you accept His gift you
can all stand before Him sin free
For one day we will all step out
of this thing called time into eternity
So on this side of life you have to prepare
for where on the other side you will be

CLEANSING TEARS

II Corinthians 12:9a And he said unto me, My grace is sufficient
for thee: for my strength is made perfect in weakness.

The joy of hearing your voice
will no longer be heard by me
For just the other day you went away
to a place that I cannot see
The memories of your smiling
face I keep deep within my heart
And I know that I am going to cry
many tears while we are apart

I thank God for the time He gave us
to share such a wonderful person as you
My life was made better because you
made a difference as you passed through
You gave something that others forgot
to give for you gave of yourself
I remember all the times you stood by
me even when there was no one else

We cannot hold on to anybody
when the Spirit of God calls unto them
No matter how much we love you
Mother the soul will always answer Him
For he has warned us that the dust
must return unto the earth again
So we must return to the earth
that place where creation first began

But Jesus promised that we should have no
fear for death will have no hold on you
So I want to just take the time to tell you
what you must in this old sinful world do
While we had a chance with the breath
in our body and the blood is still warm
We must accept Jesus as our Lord and
Saviour and then death can do us no harm

When you stepped out of my sight the other day
and with the sorrow I feel at this lost
I just wondered did the Lord God feel
this way when His own Son died on the cross
For as God in the flesh He was tested
on every point the same as you and me
Yet He chose to watch His Son suffer
and die as He became the ransom
so we could all go free

IT WAS MY APPOINTED TIME

Isaiah 57:1 THE righteous perisheth, and no man layeth it to
heart: and merciful men are taken away, none considering that the
righteous is taken away from the evil to come.

I know in your grief you will say she
was too young to have to from this life go
Never thinking that since only God sees our
tomorrows He alone knows
Of the trials and tribulations that the
adversary had in this life for her planned
But God said no and in His mercy He
called her from this old sinful land

Yes her going will be hard and painful
and of this He already in His wisdom knew
But dear one the Lord promised that no matter
how hard the trial He would never leave you
If you only could of the whole plan of God
be allowed to of His mercy in this see
That only God has the power over life and
death and He alone allowed this to be

Then you would know His plan which is written
in His Word to teach and prepare each of us
He has promised us that death has no victory
nor the grave any sting when in Him we trust
So when your time is come be ye young or in the
prime of your life or in your sunset days and are old
We will all have this date with death so if I could I
would admonish you all to prepare your soul

For dear one even your love for me no matter
how strong could not in my day hold death at bay
Just as I cannot take away the pain that you feel
at my going so again to you if I could I would say
That no man knows the day or the hour
called from life's shores to stand
Before his Maker and give an account
of the deed done in his body while living in this land

So as my day had to come so shall it come
to each and every one of you
For the dirt must return unto the earth and
the spirit to God when of this life we are through
If God allowed me one chance to you say
I would take out some soul insurance today
For when the thief known as death comes
around you will not be able to say
Lord I need more time to get my life in order
so that I can before you in peace stand
For in this life only we have the chance
to live for God so that we are assured of
peace in that eternal land

MEMORIES SO SWEET
Psalm 145:7 They shall abundantly utter the memory of thy great
goodness, and shall sing of thy righteousness.

Memories of me please keep in your minds
For they are reminders to you of days left behind
Where in my yesterdays the bright smile on my face
Will always be there to tell
that I was really in this old place

I stayed just as long as I could
and I enjoyed all my days
For memories were made so
you can remember to say
Thank God for her young life
even though it was too short for me
But remember only God in His wisdom
had the power to allow this to be

I want to remind you that I fought
the good fight and now my rest is at hand
For God said death is an appointment
from Him given to each and every man
So remember to love each other
as if it is in this life your last day
Remember tomorrow you cannot
call back and then to your loved one say
I thank God for putting you in my life
where your memories will forever stay

For tomorrow we can never be sure
if of it any of us will see
So while we have today trust
in the Lord so you will be free
And when the thief comes which is
death he will have no hold over thee
For when in this life if you put your trust
in Jesus then you can be

Assured of a place with Him in
a mansion He has prepared
Be it in death or when He returns
and you meet Him in the air
For as sure as the sun will one day set
and the moon and stars fad away
Death will come to us all so please
love each other whole heartily today

IT WAS GOD'S WILL

II Corinthians 12:9a And he said unto me, My grace is
sufficient for thee: for my strength is made perfect in
weakness.

Lord in this moment when I hurt
so bad I cannot alone stand
I hold up my heartache and say
Lord please take my hand
For I know this deep abiding pain
feels like it will never leave
And You are the only one who truly
understand so hear my plea

I come as only one can come in the midst
of this misery and such devastating pain
The love I had for my wife is a loss so great
I feel I will never truly be whole again
Friends and family gather to hold me up
but can they really of my pain understand
I know dear God that You feel my pain because
You too were tested on every point as a man

It's very hard to just accept that God
sees all and He never makes any mistakes
He alone is sovereign in absolute control no
matter whose loved one He allows death to take
So we your family and friends hold you up in
prayer and pray His strength on thee
And we thank God for the mind of going to Him
in prayer for you on our bended knees
For God hears the prayers we are privileged to
send up for you in this your time of need

HEAR MY CRY OH LORD AND DELIVER ME
Psalm 34:19 Many are the afflictions of the righteous: but the
LORD delivereth him out of them all.

My eyes gush out with the water
of sorrow that is so deep
For my mother has taken her
last breath and I just have to weep
This pain that I feel is so devastating
and so deep it feels like no other
No heartaches in life prepares us
for the pains we feel at the loss of a mother

God only lent her to us for just a very short time
The years just took off and she
is gone this sweet mother of mine
How Oh Lord can we with the loss of
our mother of this pain and heartache bear
Unless You Oh God of this burden help us
and with Your strength of it share

For God You gave us a mother to lead
and guide us most of our lives
But now she has crossed over and
we cannot see her for she is on the other side
How can we go on without her
Oh Lord please take us by the hand
Give unto us Your strength so today
we might be able to stand

Teach us Your way Oh Lord
and lead us in a plain path
For only with Your help can
we in this devastating pain last
You said in Your word that all
who labor can come unto You
For it is only with Your help
that we will of this trial get through

Yes mother is now gone but God
has promised He will never leave you alone
For He wants you all to trust Him and give
Him your lives and He will lead you home
So that when you stand before Him on tha
t awesome day at that great white throne
You can be assured of a mansion for you
He will Himself prepare
If you accept Jesus while the blood
in your body is warm for none will He spare
And only covered by His precious blood will
you have His promise that you will be God's heir

CELEBRATION OF THE LIFE OF THE
WEARY WARRIOR

Isaiah 40:1 Comfort ye, Comfort ye my people, Saith your God.

While the meadowlark was lifting
his voice singing loud and clear
The Spirit of God was calling to the
weary warrior to Him come near
This warrior had gone through
and suffered with many earthly things
But God kept His promise to this warrior
as by his side a helpmate He did bring

Together as one the Lord God fortified
them against all of the enemy's attacks
Holding onto his helpmate's hand
as she stood in the gap he never looked back
With the whole armor of God on while
his praying helpmate stood faithfully by his side
For God had promised that through these trial
this warrior would not have to alone abide

With his strong praying helpmate
by his side they learned to
Lean on God's strength for them to survive
The warrior became weary
as the banner became too heavy
So under the blood they had to continually hide

He had been called to take up
the sword of the Word of Truth
And pray as he helped many others to stand
As he became God's instrument spreading the gospel
To the lost souls in this old sin-sick land

To bring glory to the Lord this warrior was
sent to rescue many children women and men
He prayed and cried out to God for lost souls
in this special place as he refused to bend
Knowing the Master's promise that if he stood
in the gap many souls for the Lord he would win
God sent this mighty man of valor into
the parlor of death to search and find me
The Lord sent this warrior into the house
of the dead at a funeral to set me free

But now the last bell has rung for this
weary warrior and he answered the Master's call
So despite his love for his helpmate family and
friends he had to say goodbye to you all
As just the other day this weary warrior answered
the call and stepped beyond time into eternity
But he leaves a legacy of the promise if you accept
Jesus as Saviour then you too can be free

So go on and cry as you remember
the good times as well as
This time of sorrow because he had to depart
Just remember he tried to do things God's way if
sometimes he failed charge it to his head and not his heart
So dear family and loved ones God
admonished me to comfort ye
Comfort ye with these words of praise
Yes he has left us but he had made
preparations for he knew
That on his pathway to glory he
would have to pass through the grave

THIS SOUL IS MINE

Ecclesiastes 12:7 Then shall the dust return to the earth as it was: and the spirit shall return unto God who gave it.

The time of a young man's life is
not in the years he lives nor is it his to know
For death is an intricate part of life and
the Bible tells us so this we all know
Given the number of years that he spends
in this world is not the important thing
But how he lived those years and the honor
to his heavenly Father his life did bring

Using his small gifts with praise and
worship he gave God all the glory
This was really the measure of his life
and the essence of his life's story
For only God works in the hearts of men
whether they are young or old
And He alone knows the number of
our days and He seeks to save our soul

So what you see before you now is only
the dust that I left but it's not really me
For my soul is soaring so high in the heavens
for now I have truly been set free
And may the peace of the Holy Ghost
that the Father promised a Comforter to you be
So if you were given a small reprieve and the doors
of heaven would open so you could see

Then would you understand how
God could promise us that death has no sting
For when we accept Jesus in this life then
death is the pathway to life with our King
He is standing in the presence of the Lord
to receive all the promises that the Word did bring
So mother father all of the loved ones come
let us lift up our voices on high and sing

Through the tears and heartache for this young man's
life was lived to the fullest and is finished
He has all the promises that salvation can bring even
the number of years of life cannot this diminish
And the Lord God is always in control as He warned
us that death is only a pathway through the grave
He took the victory out of death and the sting out of
the grave when Jesus paid the price so we can be
saved

Remember there is no hiding place
And we know not the day or
the hour that the Father will call
The soul must answer be ye young or old
The mandate of death is appointed unto one and all

But when you make Jesus your portion
No matter the day or the hour of your appointed time
Then will God look at you through the blood of Jesus
As He did for him and say this soul is mine

GONE ON HOME

And if I go and prepare a place for you, I will come again and
receive you unto myself; that where I am, there ye may be also.
(John 14:3)

Oh Daughter of Zion Beloved of God
you fought a good fight
Although you suffered you stayed
and fought with all your might
You kept your eyes on the prize
and you were obedient and have now won
Because you put on the whole armor
for you had your faith anchored in the Holy One

The shield of faith upheld comforted and
sustained you as you kept the faith
And now you have left us and gone
on to eternity to see the Master face to face
For You believed His Word and stayed
on the King's Highway as you ran this race
God made a promise that He has kept and has
provided for you a magnificent resting place

In this life of trials and tribulations there was
much suffering as the trials were sometimes hard
But there were also great rewards
for to trust God in the midst of the trials
And follow her Saviour Jesus
was never for her too hard
Remember that this little worn out
frail body that is laying here for you to see
Can in nowise contain my spirit that is
finally soaring for now it's absolutely free

My legacy to you all is my love for God
and a life of service which was well spent
Have no fear for me because He who
has called me is where my soul is now sent
I fought a good fight and I hope that I touched
someone's life and led them to Christ
For I know that only what you do for Him
will pass the test and last past your earthly life

I know some tears will be shed but it's okay
For I had to pass through the grave and have left you
Just hold on to the Lord keep the faith and trust Him
to of this pain and sorrow bring you through

Remember you must accept Jesus as your Saviour
While your blood is warm if you plan to see me again
For I am now resting in God's
bosom and have joy unspeakable
For Him I trusted as my Saviour and friend

THE GREAT ESCAPE

. Psalm 124:7 Our soul is escaped as a bird out of the snare of the
fowlers: the snare is broken, and we are escaped

Sometimes the road seemed so very tough
No matter how hard I tried it was never enough
My life was of much heartache and of problems so full
Until one day at the foot of the cross I stood

On that blessed day so long ago
I made my peace with Almighty God
No matter what occurred my life
no longer in the muck had need to plod
I am a child of the King and heir
to all the promises it brings
For while the breath was in me I
chose Jesus above all worldly things

And now I have His assurance that
He alone will show me the way
For no other name under the sun
could deliver my soul past the grave
But with His covenant of eternity
as a promise to me Jesus gave
When I offered Him my life
and on that glorious day I was saved

Although death really doesn't have
any authority over me
We all know that death is the
way sin caused it to be
Please remember that this earthly
house you now see
Had to die so that now with the Master
I can be totally free

Keep in mind that while the blood
was warm in me I chose
To give my life to Jesus
who is the Master of my soul
Shed a few tears then go on
with your lives as you must
Rejoicing always because you
know that in God I put all my trust

Remember that we will meet
again just inside the pearly gates
As you give your lives to the Master
you will also share my fate
For in this old sinful world my work
as a witness for the Lord is finally done
I have with peace and joy laid down my life
to wake in the morning in the bosom of the Son

THESE TREASURES IN EARTHEN VESSALS

Jeremiah 29:11 For I know the thoughts that I think toward you,
saith the LORD, thoughts of peace, and not of evil, to give you an
expected end.

I know the thoughts I have toward you saith the Lord
One day you will understand for
it will not be for you too hard
I laid down my life so that you could be free
For sin caused a separation of you from Me

So as sin came into the world I executed My plan
That through the pathway of the grave you could stand
For the treasure that I placed into you
with my own sweet breath
Housed a treasure that the enemy
tried to steal through death

But the soul would always seek
its Master and of Him answer the call
For Jesus the Saviour said come unto me
for I have ransomed you yes I paid it all
So when you hear that last trump of God
calling you be not afraid for you have the victory
As long ago the sacrificial Lamb of God took
the sting from death when he hung on that cursed tree

So death is not an enemy of the saints
because it is the pathway on our way home
And we have the Lord's blessed assurance
we will not have to take this journey alone
For as the Holy Ghost will for us
light the way to our mansion in eternity
And Jesus will meet us there as
He is our propitiator the One who died to set us free